Take The Lead
The Need For Breed

By
Scott Harrington (DTC-CDT)

Take The Lead The Need For Breed

Author: Scott Harrington

Copyright © 2025 Scott Harrington

The right of Scott Harrington to be identified as author of this work has been asserted by the author in accordance with section 77 and 78 of the Copyright, Designs and Patents Act 1988.

First Published in 2025

ISBN 978-1-83538-391-9 (Paperback)
      978-1-83538-392-6 (E-Book)

Book Cover Design and Book Layout by:
    White Magic Studios
    www.whitemagicstudios.co.uk

Published by:
    Maple Publishers
    Fairbourne Drive, Atterbury,
    Milton Keynes,
    MK10 9RG, UK
    www.maplepublishers.com

A CIP catalogue record for this title is available from the British Library.

All rights reserved. No part of this book may be reproduced or translated in any form or by any means, electronic or mechanical, including photocopying, recording or by any information storage and retrieval system without written permission from the author.

The views expressed in this work are solely those of the author/editor and do not reflect the opinions of Publishers, and the Publisher hereby disclaims any responsibility for them.

Contents

Introduction 4

Chapter 1 – Terriers 6

Chapter 2 – Working Dogs 16

Chapter 3 – Gun Dogs 31

Chapter 4 – Utility Dogs 49

Chapter 5 – Hounds 61

Chapter 6 – Pastoral Dogs 83

Chapter 7 – Toy Dogs 103

Chapter 8 – Cross Breeds - Bonus Chapter 116

Acknowledgments 128

About the Author 130

Introduction

Dogs are the most friendly sidekick any kid could have! They can be great friends to us humans because of their bubbly social nature and loyalty. Evolving from wolves, dogs were the first animal species to be domesticated and bred by humans into multiple breed groups to perform jobs that play to their strengths. This means that instead of being out in the wild, dogs evolve into the companions we know and love today. They've gone from roaming in the wild to playing fetch in the park, which is pretty cool when you think about how far the species has evolved. Just like us, dogs have their own skills and talents to offer. Us humans are all good at different things and you've probably wondered why your best friend is good at one subject while you are better at another. Dogs are exactly the same in this aspect. They are individuals with unique traits and characteristics that make them who they are. The important thing is finding a dog that has similar characteristics so they can live in harmony with you. Afterall, it's commonly said that 'dogs are a reflection of their owner.' We all love nothing more than resting our brains after a long day of learning at school. For you, this might look like playing out with friends or catching up with our favourite cartoons. Dogs need this kind of entertainment too, but in a more K9-friendly way (unless of course, your dog does enjoy the odd cartoon!). One of the most important things for them is to keep their minds stimulated through training and enriching activities. This is known as a special power called breed fulfilment, which you will learn all about here to enrich your dog's life. In this book, we will discuss not only how all dogs should be walked and given physical exercise, but also mental stimulation. Many dogs are great pets, but the happiest dogs in the world are the ones who are using their natural abilities and doing what they were bred for. So if you're excited to learn more about being the best dog owner and giving your pet the most fun-filled life possible for them, let's take a look at some of these wonderful dog breeds in their categories and learn more about the fun activities we can offer to make them happy pups.

Something to note is how we all have a preference in the types of dogs we like to surround ourselves with. Many families choose Terriers as K9 companions for typically being small breeds. Never underestimate the Terriers, they are little dogs with big-dog attitudes.

These feisty dogs were bred to defend their territory against vermin (little creatures like rats and mice). Terriers could practically run their own pest control business they were that useful. Many Terrier breeds display great ability to chase away pest intruders by digging underground. It's vital that Terrier dog owners fully appreciate the high energy and stubbornness that comes with these hardy workaholic dogs. It is often mistaken that Terriers are quiet and easy, but they need a lot of activity much like bigger dogs.

THE STAFFORDSHIRE BULL TERRIER

The Staffordshire Bull Terrier is an extremely popular dog to own. 'Staffies' have impeccable trainability and show loyalty to their owners, always eager to please. They are known as the nanny dogs for their love and gentleness towards children. Like many Terriers, Staffies can be stubborn if not trained confidently by the owner. There is a prejudice against Staffies though for being dangerous dogs, in the early 2000's there was a public panic encouraged by the news, that Staffies were not safe dogs to have as pets. Over the years, this has been proven wrong as Staffies became family protectors and we have more knowledge of how to keep them happy. These strong powerful dogs were originally bred for bullbaiting and even fighting sports. Agility activities, like hurdles and jumping are recommended as breed fulfilment for Staffies. With this breed, sometimes a standard walk just isn't enough to keep their muscles healthy. They need more, so an active owner happy to be on the go would be the best fit. Another enriching activity for the powerful Staffordshire Bull Terrier would be a long-lasting chew, either with a toy or specialist chew-bones from the pet shop.

THE JACK RUSSELL TERRIER

The Jack Russell is an enthusiastic as well as energetic Terrier that can be very loyal to its owner, but once again stubborn. Jack Russells are easily bored when not given enough exercise and mental stimulation. They are a breed that is underestimated in need, and often are put with owners that cannot fit their needs for this reason. It's important to utilise their energy and to make sure your lifestyle provides them with suitable breed-fulfilling activities such as going on long runs together in the fresh air or even physical sports that will teach them agility. Dock diving is known to be enriching and rewarding for a Jack Russell; fearlessly jumping from a ledge to swim and retrieve an item for their loving family. You could even simulate the Jack Russell Terrier's original job chasing away pests by making them chase their toys. There's a brilliant dog sport called "Flyball" where dogs race across obstacles to retrieve a ball attached to a spring and straight back again over the obstacles. What Terrier wouldn't enjoy that?

THE BORDER TERRIER

Border Terriers have earned their name from the environment they were originally bred to work in based on the border of Scotland & England. They would hunt the likes of otters, badgers & foxes. While the Border Terrier is a busy breed, they are also 'cheeky chappies' and know how to have fun while they are working, they are very much work hard and play hard type dogs! These Terriers can be very affectionate and sociable as long as they are appropriately habituated and socialised with various animals at a young age, otherwise their natural chasing instincts can get the better of them. Due to their intelligence and trainability, Border Terriers can sometimes be too smart for their own good. Because of this, it's important to start training as soon as possible and introduce plenty of fulfilment activities. While the Border Terrier, like all dogs, needs physical exercise on walks, you can add variety by going on long adventure hikes, or maybe visit a suitable area to allow them to explore and even dig. A simple game of fetch or tug of war can also be a lot of fun and enriching for a Border Terrier.

THE AIREDALE TERRIER

Onto a slightly larger dog, the Airedale has been nicknamed the king of Terriers. Originally bred in the mid-1800s, the Airedale Terrier evolved from a mix of the Otter Hound, Old English Black & Tanned Terrier and the English Bull Terrier to create the most versatile hunting Terrier breed. The Airedale's original job was to hunt small or large vermin either digging them out or swimming in pursuit of otters. English farmers at the time needed a good multipurpose hunting dog to deal with a variety of pests, small, large, underground or on the waterways. Airedale Terriers have adapted from this need to be the dogs we know and love today. Airedale Terriers can be very loving family companions and also excel in hunting. It's been said they possess the hunting skills of a Pointer, Spaniel and Retriever all in one dog. Many Airedale Terriers served in World War I, carrying messages from the commanding officers to the trenches, as well as guarding the camps against pests. As the Airedale is truly a jack of all trades, there are so many activities you can do to keep an Airedale stimulated, from agility to hunting sports, swimming and fetch to name a few.

THE YORKSHIRE TERRIER

Over to one of the smallest Terriers of all, the Yorkshire Terrier! 'Yorkies' stand approximately 8 inches tall and are full of personality, making them a big dog trapped in a small-body constantly seeking excitement. Though Yorkies are considered to be more of a 'Toy dog' than a Terrier, they were originally bred to work on the Yorkshire farms and chase away vermin similar size to themselves. Yorkshire Terriers can coexist nicely with children and other animals with firm training and strong socialisation at an early age. To really make these tiny firework-like pups happy, a simple game of tug of war or fetch is an ultimate mood booster. Another great activity for Yorkies is to mix up their walks and give them new areas to explore, they love adventure.

THE WEST HIGHLAND TERRIER

West Highland Terriers display very strong playful personalities, in addition to their original job to hunt in Argyleshire, Scotland. 'Westies' were bred like many terriers to help farmers reduce infestation against pests. This magnificent Terrier was evolved from the Dandie Dinmont Terrier, the Skye Terrier, the Scottish Terrier and the Cairn Terrier all to create a small hunting terrier with the full package. Westies proved to be exceptionally good at chasing away small rodents to bigger wildlife like foxes. These polar bear-like dogs are recognised by their bright white coats which was handy to help the owners separate the dog from the prey it was hunting. Westies are likely to get along perfectly in a family environment, but not so much around other small animal pets such as hamsters or rabbits. This is due to their strong Terrier prey drive. Along with tug of war or at times, agility, Westies are avid football fans who love nothing more than a good kick about in the park, much like many of you, I'm sure! This is most likely as it simulates their original job to chase, almost making it like a fun practice game for them.

THE TIBETAN TERRIER

Though their name suggests Terrier, the Tibetan Terrier got their name from Europeans who thought the breed resembled Terriers within their appearance. Tibetan Terriers these days are classed as Utility Dogs. They were originally bred in ancient Tibet in the 20th century and used by Tibetan Monks to herd sheep. A much historical evolution to what we associate them with now. Tibetan Terriers are excellent family dogs for being gentle and loyal towards their loved ones, as well as being very playful and sociable with other dogs. As Tibetan Terriers are very eager to please their loving leaders, these dogs can be very easy to train. The intense love and loyalty Tibetan Terriers have for their owners can make them prone to separation anxiety. Puzzles are recommended for enrichment, a Tibetan Terrier will fully invest in working out snuffle mats and various other puzzle toys whenever they are feeling lonely. Though it's important that a Tibetan Terrier gets exercise on walks like all dogs, they can also really enjoy training activities and learning new tricks. Owners of a Tibetan Terrier may also find competitive sports such as dog shows and agility fun activities to keep these fluffy pups happy.

WHAT HAVE YOU LEARNED ABOUT TERRIERS? Terriers are highly energetic and intelligent dogs that can be fantastic companions, providing they get plenty of exercise in addition to problem solving through toys. As well as having lots of playtime chasing things, particularly other high energy dogs when socialised properly.

QUIZ

DO YOU KNOW YOUR TERRIER?

Which terriers are known as 'Nanny' Dogs?

Which Terriers are often called 'Toy Dogs?'

What do Terriers normally chase?

This chapter is devoted to some rather large dogs that you've probably seen out and about. A lot of the most ancient dog breeds in the world belong to the working group and are still seen today doing the same jobs, such as assisting humans, guarding and herding. These dogs are typically known for being large and powerful which may not be suitable for every household. But with that quality in mind, working dogs come in a variety of temperaments that can make them suitable companions for a variety of different personas.

THE BERNESE MOUNTAIN DOG

The Bernese Mountain Dog is among the most popular working dogs, making them a popular choice in family homes. These 'gentle giants' have been used as search and rescue dogs and even therapy dogs, making them devoted and loyal K9 companions. Originating from Bern, Switzerland, the Bernese Mountain Dog was originally used for a variety of tasks to assist humans, from cattle herding to even pulling dairy carts to the markets. These dogs are very strong weighing around 50kg. Despite their large appearance, they have beautiful personalities that cannot be denied. What makes Bernese Mountain Dogs perfect pets is their affectionate personality and docile attitude while at home. Despite being domesticated in this destination, it is very important to remember that working dogs like the Bernese Mountain dog still need mental stimulation through enrichment activities provided by their loving leaders. Much like you! We all like to spend time at home, but without visiting the playground or having days out, we become rather bored. For Bernese Mountain Dogs, these activities should include agility. As an activity for you to join in on, you could create an obstacle course for you both to enjoy. Another excellent game for a Bernese Mountain Dog could be scent searching games to simulate their job to rescue people. This type of game is so productive and also helps support a bonding experience between you and your dog.

THE BOXER DOG

Despite their harsh looking exterior, The Boxer is an extremely fun dog to own as a pet as they are the comedians of the K9 world! Boxers are very energetic and playful dogs who love nothing more than to have lots of fun with their owners. A boxer needs very patient training, so be sure to be consistent in training whilst maintaining a good sense of humour for them to enjoy. While Boxers rarely show signs of aggression, it's important to socialise them early as they can be wary of strangers. Socialising means to get them used to certain environments. We are socialised as children into learning by being taught by our families and then later, at school. By getting them used to strangers and other dogs early, you will have an easier task whilst out on walks later on. Boxers were bred in 19th-century Germany as hunting dogs and later used for bullbaiting. Boxers also worked to assist butchers to control cattle. They got their name from the personality trait of playing and standing on their hind legs to box other dogs or people, whilst also making a snorting noise, this is because they are prone to developing Obstructed Airways Syndrome due to their flat noses. Obstructed Airways Syndrome is when the passage of air struggles to get into the upper respiratory system because of a dog's genetic makeup. It's very similar to humans who suffer with asthma or chest problems, because they often have to spend more time catching their breath and being that bit more careful. Despite this fact, Boxers need plenty of exercise like all dogs, but they can really benefit from having these walks mixed up from time to time by going on long hikes or occasionally shorter walks in new places as well as swimming. A good retrieving game with a frisbee can also be endless fun for a Boxer and it's owner.

THE NEWFOUNDLAND

Another gentle giant in the working dog fraternity is the Newfoundland. Known as the world's most powerful water dog breed, the Newfoundland is one of the greatest lifeguards you'll ever meet. 'Newfies' got their name from their origin in Newfoundland, Canada. These giant teddy bear-like dogs were bred to help fishermen in the 16th century by using their tremendous strength to pull the boats in and out of the docks. Newfies can be perfect companions to own with their strong empathy and loyalty, but they must have a job to remain happy dogs. It's no secret that Newfies are sublime swimmers with their thick double coats for water resistance and webbed paws, ergo dock diving and other swim retrieving activities can be the perfect breed-fulfilling games for Newfoundlands.

THE SIBERIAN HUSKY

Known for being one of the most wolf-like and oldest dog breeds on the planet is the Siberian Husky. Bred by the ancient spiritual hunting community of Siberia, the Siberian Husky was originally used as a hunting dog when the native land had warmer temperatures. As the years went by, the temperatures dropped and the people of Siberia had to move on, carrying their belongings and families together. This changed the Husky from a hunting dog to a travelling dog, pulling the sledges of Siberian families. As time went by in the breed's travels, the Husky's talents in sledge pulling were discovered by a Russian fur trader named William Goosak, who brought the breed over to Nome, Alaska to take part in the 1909 All Alaska Sweepstakes, a 408-mile dog sledding race with a $10,000 cash price. Goosak's team of Huskies came in 3rd place. Although the Husky didn't win their first sledding race, this was the beginning of their legacy. Many dog breeders were impressed with the Husky's talent for sled racing which was at the time not expected, so much so that more Huskies were bred as they grew in popularity. The following years of the All Alaska Sweepstakes saw umpteen Husky entries, leading to the Siberian Husky becoming the go-to breed for the sport. As Huskies are active dogs, the ideal owner for a Husky must live quite an active life. Hiking and exploring new areas can be fun for Huskies, but when it comes to sporting activities, agility is the perfect hobby for you and your Siberian Husky, unless you live in a cold snowy climate, in which case a Husky will thoroughly enjoy sled pulling. You will know Huskies today as the predominantly blue and grey eyed fluffy dogs that resemble wolves.

THE ENGLISH MASTIFF

Holding the record as the heaviest dog on the planet is the English Mastiff! These gigantic dogs can weigh up to 91kg! Though originally bred in England as one of the oldest dog breeds in history, the English Mastiff was taken to ancient Rome by the Romans to bait lions, tigers and bears in the Roman arenas. This just demonstrates their power. English Mastiffs were used as hunting dogs, but would never kill their prey, but rather hold them down and restrain them when captured using their colossal strength. English Mastiffs have also been used as intimidation guard dogs to protect wealthy homes of their livestock. Similarly, Bull Mastiffs were also bred as guard dogs for the wealthiest of dog owners. Both the Bull & English Mastiff dogs display calm and affectionate personalities and are both loyal to their owners. Though these dogs would happily sleep for most of their time, they will find the energy to work when needed. Breed-fulfilling activities for both the Bull & English Mastiff can include a gentle stroll and explore new areas to maybe even letting them dig. Obedience and dog show training activities can also be fun for both the dogs and their owners. At times these gentle giants may not wish to mobilise as much as other dogs, and that's when a good puzzle like a snuffle mat can really be useful.

THE GREAT DANE

If you've seen Scooby Doo, you will be familiar with this breed: the Great Dane. Known for being one of the tallest and largest dogs in the world, the Great Dane's original purpose was to hunt large animals such as bears, deer and even wild boar. The tallest Great Dane on record stood up to almost 4 feet tall, that could be as tall as you! It has been believed that similar dogs that would evolve into today's Great Dane came from existing back as far as Ancient Greece and Ancient Egypt. Although the breed originated in 16th Century Germany initially. Great Danes are much softer and more gentle than they look, but might not be suitable for every household due to their size. Just one swing of their tails can be powerful enough to damage valuable objects. If you're a household that is particularly precious about sentimental items, a Great Dane could be a risk for you. It can also be challenging to bring these large dogs out to public places if there is a limited amount of space, so it's a breed where you have to be mindful and organised ahead of time. Great Danes enjoy going on gentle walks or even jogging, but two particular activities that Great Danes will always love are obstacle courses to build up their athleticism and fitness levels along with retrieving a toy in the park or even kicking around a football.

THE SAINT BERNARD

Now onto a very large dog that is often referred to as the ultimate superhero: the Saint Bernard. They originated in the western Alps of Switzerland, bred to perform search and rescue operations, whilst carrying a small barrel of brandy around their collar. This was to be given to lost victims in the snow to keep warm while awaiting further recovery. This helpful nature has adapted with them over time, making them considerate and empathetic dogs with excellent sense of their owner's needs. The Saint Bernard would work in packs by searching for people lost in the snow and keeping them warm by surrounding them with their warm fur, whilst other dogs would run away in search of help. The Saint Bernards that were originally working in the brutal winters of the 17th century showed immense dedication to their jobs, putting their own lives at risk in avalanches. It's safe to say any good owner of a Saint Bernard must show these beautiful dogs lots of respect by giving them plenty of enrichment activities and praise. These activities could be difficult to find, however, there are some very simple ways to make a Saint Bernard very happy. It's vital to schedule some well-earned relaxing downtime. While you and your Saint Bernard are taking a pleasant walk together, find somewhere comfy like a bench to just sit and do nothing. Saint Bernards love their relaxation, but rather than just do it at home, take them outside in the fresh air with new views and smells to take in. Another fun activity would be to replicate their search and rescue operations by doing mantrailing, conditioning the dog to search for someone specific.

THE ROTTWEILER

One of the most popular breeds of working dogs is the Rottweiler. These breeds are known for their dedication in trying to please their owner. Similar to the Staffordshire Bull Terrier, the Rottweiler can sometimes get a bad reputation due to moral panics from the media in the early 2000s. What they really are though are phenomenal companions. This is of course, if they are well bred, in the right hands and socialised properly from an early age. 'Rotties' were originally bred in Germany as guard dogs for the upper class. They were a status symbol for wealth and prosperity, a whole world away from the reputation they often receive now. Rottweilers initially evolved from the ancient fighting dogs used by the Romans to guard their livestock as well as take on the enemy in battles. Rotties are one of the best guard dogs for families on account of their loyalty. Case Study on Rotties: A famous Rottweiler from Coventry named Jake protected a stranger from being attacked. Jake alerted his owner to the crime and then held down the attacker, waiting for the police to arrive.

Jake became a national hero in the UK being the epitome of what a good Rottweiler should be. Rottweilers are all about fairness and justice, they have no patience for any kind of cruelty to those who don't deserve it.

Working dogs are big and powerful B.F.G's (big friendly giants) that need their exercise and plenty of activity. Despite this, it's highly recommended to be creative when replicating their original jobs. Enrichment toys such as snuffle mats combined with obstacle courses can really make working dogs happy and at peace with their loving owners. Although beautiful to look at, these dogs are not for the faint of heart and need owners that can prioritise and adapt them into every day routines.

QUIZ

Which dog is scooby doo based off?

Which dog is currently holding the record for heaviest dog?

Which dog originated from Bern, Switzerland?

Gun Dogs are a collection of breeds that are naturally active. Their biological characteristics make them helpful companions for sporting activities. Dogs in the Gun Dog group were all bred to assist hunters in the tracking and retrieving of feathered game. Feathered game means wild birds and animals that are hunted. Gun Dogs are split into Retrievers, Spaniels, Setters and Pointers, also known as HPR (Hunt Point Retrieve.) These dogs are known for their brilliant temperaments as well as their eager drive to work and please their owners. Though many Gun Dogs have lots in common, they also come in a variety of shapes and sizes with different talents when it comes to hunting jobs.

THE LABRADOR-RETRIEVER

The Labrador-Retriever is a noble Gun Dog that can be excellent for families to own. Evolving from the now-extinct Saint John's Water Dog or Lesser Newfoundland, Labrador-Retrievers first appeared during the 1700's. Early Labradors worked as retriever dogs for the Canadian fishermen out in the Labrador Sea. Their job was to jump in the water and retrieve any rogue fish that had escaped through the nets. As the years went by, British 2nd Earl of Malmesbury James Harris took a shining to what was then known as the Saint John's Water Dog when visiting Newfoundland. He brought the breed over to Britain in the 1800s to set out and develop them into shooting companions for hunters. In addition to James Harris, the 5th Duke of Beccleuch Walter Scott was also developing a gundog breed from some of the Newfoundland retriever dogs he had brought back to Britain. Walter Scott named his dogs Labrador dogs. James Harris and Walter Scott knew about each other during this time. Jumping forward some years later, the sons of both James Harris and Walter Scott met each other on a shoot day. The two sons put their heads together and bred two male Labrador dogs from Malmesbury with two Buccleuch kennel females, officially creating the Labrador-Retriever that we know today. In America, the Labrador-Retriever holds the record for being the most registered dog breed since 1991. While Labradors are popular hunting dogs retrieving pheasants and various waterfowl on shoot days, they have also been adaptive enough to be used as guide dogs for the blind. Some Labradors also work as therapy dogs, providing emotional support for their owners. Although they have a useful nature, they are friendly to their core, making them a perfect family pet.

THE GOLDEN RETRIEVER

Very similar to the Labrador is the Golden Retriever. Originally bred in the Scottish highlands by Dudley Marjoribanks the 1st Baron of Tweedmouth who wanted to create the 'new improved Labrador.' Dudley took what was known as the Yellow Retriever mixed with Hounds, Setters and the Tweed Water Spaniel. It took over 50 years to eventually create what is now known as the Golden Retriever. Dudley's goal was to create a breed that would display all the best qualities of the Labrador-Retriever and add more water resistance with their thick, golden double coats. Golden Retrievers are another breed of dog that has been used for retrieving and assisting the blind as guide dogs and also working as therapy dogs.

THE FLAT-COATED RETRIEVER

Though it has been believed that the Flat-Coated Retriever evolved from the Golden Retriever, the two key ancestors of the Flat-Coated Retriever are the Newfoundland and the Labrador-Retriever. Flat-Coated Retrievers display energetic and playful personalities that the majority of people love. Similar to the Boxer, it's important for owners to maintain a level of patience and a good sense of humour. While the Flat-Coated Retriever was bred as a retriever dog for both water and land game, 'Flatties' have also displayed great talent for flushing out game from cover on shoot days and have even been used to sniff out illegal substances with the American Police, helping to solve cases!

THE NOVA SCOTIA DUCK TOLLING RETRIEVER

A very popular Gun Dog in the Canadian Kennel Club is the Nova Scotia Duck Tolling Retriever. Known for being one of the smallest retriever dogs, 'Tollers' have a similar appearance to the Golden Retriever's copper/golden coats with some white streaks along the body and face. During the 19th century, both British and Canadian hunters were developing K9 companions to retrieve feathered game on land and water. This is how the Nova was originally bred, in eastern Canada from a mix of Cocker Spaniel, Irish Setter and English Shepherd. The Nova Scotia Duck Tolling Retriever had a unique way of assisting hunters. They did this by luring feathered game closer to the shore as the dog splashed around in the water. They would swim out and retrieve game later when told by hunters. Like many retrievers, Tollers are very sociable dogs that make wonderful pets for families with children; however, they love the sound of their voice and can be very vocal dogs.

THE CHESAPEAKE BAY RETRIEVER

With a similar prey drive to Tollers and Labradors, the Chesapeake Bay Retriever is another water dog that was originally bred to retrieve waterfowl for hunters. This time originating from Maryland, Chesapeake Bay. Spaniels, Hounds and the Saint John's Water Dog are believed to be the ancestors of these particular dogs. 'Chessys' resemble the Labrador Retriever but with wiry coats in colours such as chocolate and gold. Chessys can be stubborn at times and require their owners to be consistent with training and  are best suited to people who are active with on the go lifestyles. It's fair to say that all retrievers are full of life and love nothing more than to please their owners and get lots of love in return. For each of the above dogs, many breed-fulfilling activities include fetching and retrieving games. This is a great training opportunity to teach them to wait and retrieve on command. This gives them a skill at impulse control in addition to fetching toys. Dock diving is another great way to replicate their original jobs to retrieve fish or waterfowl by letting them jump in the water and swim to retrieve a ball or dummy. On hot days when it's recommended to keep dogs indoors, enrichment puzzles such as snuffle mats can be fantastic mental stimulation.

THE WELSH SPRINGER SPANIEL

Onto the Spaniels now and let's start with the oldest breed recognised, the Welsh Springer Spaniel. This very affectionate Gun Dog was bred as a hunting dog in the 17th Century in Wales and later replaced by the Cocker and English Springer Spaniels. The name Springer Spaniel comes from the 'Welshie's' bouncy style of flushing out feathered game from hiding places. The Welshie's extremely energetic nature was utilised for long, tiring shoot days. Welshies can be difficult to train by the fact that they are excitable puppies that maintain this level of intense happiness. This does go into adulthood and makes them a wonderful pet, but can be difficult to sustain rules and training early on.

THE ENGLISH SPRINGER SPANIEL

The English Springer Spaniel is one of the oldest Gun Dogs in Europe that is still popular to own even to this day. They were originally bred in Shropshire, England. Much like the Welsh Springer Spaniel, English Springers are highly energetic hunters who love to impress their owners. Like all Spaniels, Springers have a gifted sense of smell when it comes to tracking game. Although it was their original job to blow the cover of feathered game by flushing them out for the hunters, Springers  have also been used for retrieving game after they track it down. After clocking off from a hard day's work in the fields, Springers love to switch off and relax in the comfort of their home with their loving families. Springers have been used in the police force as sniffer dogs, assisting officers in searching criminals for illegal substances and stolen goods with the help of their powerful noses. While many Retriever dogs have worked assisting the blind, Springers make impeccable assistance dogs to help people with physical disabilities like the many wonderful humans who work as carers.

THE COCKER SPANIEL

Objectively, the most popular Spaniel dog to own is the beautiful Cocker Spaniel, believed to be originally bred in Spain where the Spaniel name comes from. However, the most modern Cocker that we all know and love today came from the UK in 1850. Another superb Gun Dog used for flushing out game and sniffing out for prey on shoots. A prestigious dog show known as Crufts has seen the Cocker Spaniel win umpteen competitions more times than any other dog breed in the world! Cockers are very popular dogs to be owned by families with children due to their cuddly and affectionate nature. However, it is very important to remember that all Spaniels were bred to work and must be given the best breed fulfilment activities to keep them happy. All Spaniels can be excellent in many of the same retrieving activities for the retriever dogs. Many Spaniels can gain a lot of mental stimulation from snuffle mats and man-trailing as it allows them to use their natural sniff tracking abilities. Agility is a fun activity for both Spaniels and owners to enjoy together. Agility can be one of the best thrilling activities for dogs as active as Spaniels.

THE ENGLISH SETTER

Among the more elegant Gun Dogs are the Setter breeds such as the glorious English Setter. The English Setter is a medium-sized Gun Dog with a medium-length white double coat, peppered with dark spots and patches. They are one of the oldest gun dog breeds in the UK dating all the way back to the 15th century and were originally known as the Setting Spaniel. English Setters were bred and used for crouching, pointing and retrieving feathered game such as quails and pheasants for aristocratic hunters in England. They also put their water-resistant coats to good use when retrieving waterfowl. English Setters are much like the Welsh Springer Spaniel with energetic and playful personalities but require plenty of patience when training. Their demeanour is loving and affectionate towards their owners making them great companions for families with children.

THE IRISH SETTER

So much about the English Setter can equally be said about the Red Irish Setter. Irish Setters are one of the most striking gun dogs to look at with their superb long red coats, making them very popular Gun Dogs to own as pets. During the 19th Century, the Irish Setter was originally bred in Rossmore Castle, County Monaghan from the previous mix of Red & White Setters. Nowadays Irish Setters are used as champion show dogs in Crufts. Irish Setters have also been known to work as therapy dogs along with some of the Retreiver breeds.

THE GORDON SETTER

Another setter with a beautiful appearance is the black & tan Gordon Setter, also known as the black avenger of the highlands. The Gordon Setter is the heaviest of the Setter breeds weighing between 45 to 80 pounds. Gordon Setters get their name from the 4th Duke of Gordon, Alexander Gordon in the 18th century, who gained a preference to these dogs for their hunting abilities. Gordon Setters are devoted to their owners but can be unsure of strangers if not given proper training. All Setters love to retrieve, making a game of fetch one of the many perfect breed-fulfilling activities for these amazing gun dogs. It's also a great idea to test their brains and make them wait and retrieve on your command as their leader. Dogs as active as Setters can also benefit from taking on the sport of agility and even dog shows.

THE GERMAN POINTER

Over to the final group of Gun Dogs the pointing fraternity, and who better to start us off than the magnificent German Pointer! Pointers are one of the most athletic working companions in the Gun Dog arena. These dogs are extremely energetic and fairly easy to train, their energy is on the next level up from the typical Labrador. German Pointers were originally bred in 19th Century Germany as hunting dogs on land and water. Pointers along with the Setters were very popular shooting companions for the upper class. They were bred to be perfect multi-purpose hunting dogs for tracking retrieving and of course, pointing. All Pointer dogs display a unique style of hunting with their sublime eyesight and will stop in a tense position and point towards feathered game. Pointers have short doublecoats for water resistance and can come in black, liver and even a mix of brown and white. While German Pointers have been used to hunt the typical game on shoots such as pheasants, pigeons and waterfowl, they have also been capable of hunting possums, boars and even deer. Along with Spaniels, German Pointers have proven to be useful in assisting the police by sniffing out illegal substances and stolen goods.

THE HUNGARIAN VIZSLA

An incredibly similar dog to the German Pointer with the same loyal, affectionate qualities and strong working drive is the Hungarian Vizsla. Bred in the Puszta region of Hungary, the Vizsla displays a virtually identical physical appearance to the Pointer but with a short, dense coat in a fox red colour. Although they are also athletic hunting dogs like Pointers, Vizslas are slightly less energetic making them better suited to owners who are less active. Both Pointers and Vizslas love their owners so much and are very extroverted dogs who can get lonely easily.

THE WEIMARANER

And finally onto one of the most distinctive-looking Gun Dogs in the world the Weimaraner! Known as the grey ghost, the Weimaraner was originally bred during the late 18th century in what was then known as the city of Weimar, now the state of Thuringia, central Germany as a hunting dog to track down large game such as bears, boars and deer. Weimaraners are excellent multi-purpose Gun Dogs who can be great, affectionate pets and very pretty to look at with their silver coats. They truly love to work and are very much athletes in the K9 world. Though less vocal and more gentle than the Hungarian Vizsla, Weimaraners can at times be stubborn and hard to train when not given the appropriate breed fulfilment at an optimum level. This can be said for all the HPR dogs. These activities can include retrieving on both land and water, man-trailing to give a simulation of tracking on a shoot day, and the always popular agility to feed a HPR dog's athletic needs with obstacles thrown in for a challenge. In conclusion, Gun Dogs are very energetic and loyal dogs with so many wonderful qualities to offer! It's highly recommended to sign these incredible dogs up for Gun-Dog classes and learn about their origins and purpose and then replicate the original jobs of Gun Dogs to let them happily use all their natural abilities and receive love and praise in return.

QUIZ

Which region of Hungary do the Vizsla dogs come from?

Which century do German pointer dogs originate from?

Where do English Springer Spaniels originate from?

Which dog is so excitable as a puppy they can be hard to train?

There is no breed group harder to generalise than the Utility group due to the wide variety of different dogs with varying backgrounds. Most breeds in the Utility group nowadays are used simply as companion dogs, but that's not to say they don't have their individual personalities and origins. We'll go over all the brilliant dogs in this chapter that may be Utility Dogs, but have different advantages to owning and loving.

THE POODLE

The Poodle is a very elegant looking pooch, but they have an interesting backstory. Alongside the Siberian Husky, Poodles are one of the oldest dog breeds in the world, records of the breed can be traced back to ancient Rome. In Rome, Poodles were originally used as hunting dogs and in 15th century France, they were used as water retrievers like the Labrador. This was due to their curly hair being excellent for water resistance. Poodles became more associated with elegance and class and they are even believed to be the first performing dogs in theatre and circus acts. Being an upper class, socialite of a dog, this led to a more artistic correlation to the breed. Many Poodles appeared in paintings and sculptures with their loving owners during the 17th century. Poodles can come in a variety of sizes standing from just 10 inches tall to 30 inches. They are also one of the most intelligent dogs to train making them versatile for a variety of jobs, including the American military during the Second World War carrying messages alongside the Airedale Terrier. Poodles have even worked as assistance dogs for the disabled just like Labradors and Golden Retrievers. These days, you will often find poodles and mixed breeds of poodles as emotional support dogs for owners who are neurodivergent or struggle with anxiety. For a breed with many talents as well as high intelligence, Poodles can really benefit with continuous training and learning new tricks to keep their clever minds engaged. This can come from dog shows, obedience training programs, agility and even gundog classes.

THE BRITISH BULLDOG

A very popular Utility Dog with its distinctive personality and notorious wobbly cheeks is the British Bulldog. Though intimidating at first sight, Bulldogs are sweet and gentle K9s that can be the perfect choice for families. Especially those that are longing for the companionship of a dog but can't tend to any that are high maintenance. Bulldogs are one of the easiest breeds to own and are ideal for this reason. Bulldogs originally evolved from the Mastiff dogs used for bull baiting in Ancient Rome, hence their name "Bulldog". Once the breed was brought over to England and officially recognised by the kennel club as the British Bulldog, the bull baiting skills were developed into baiting badgers during the 1800's. The British Bulldog that we know today has been bred to serve simply as a loving companion.

Much like the Staffordshire Bull Terrier, British Bulldogs coexist nicely with children and other domestic pets. Bulldogs come in a fairly medium height and size, though it is worth reminding that although they are low maintenance dogs, they still require physical exercise as they can be prone to gaining weight. All dogs are sensitive to hot temperatures, but the Bulldog in particular can easily overheat. This is due to their flat noses causing Obstructed Airways Syndrome, so be sure to provide shade and plenty of water during the summer holidays. When it comes to activities to entertain Bulldogs, their chilled disposition makes them willing to try anything. Bulldogs are not energetic, however a simple tug of war game with their favourite toy can bring them joy as well as many water games. Treat your Bulldog to a shallow paddling pool to splash around in with excitement. Did you know that Bulldogs have become known to be naturally good at skateboarding? In recent years there have been many viral videos uploaded to the internet of Bulldogs gliding around on skateboards. You may have even seen them! This talent comes from their short and stubby legs and barrel chests giving them the perfect and natural ability to move their weight and steer themselves as they roll along.

THE DALMATIAN

Onto a Utility Dog that we all know from the Disney movie 101 Dalmatians, the spotty Dalmatian is also a Utility Dog that is incredibly popular. They were originally bred to lead firefighter carriages through the streets on their way to put out fires and clear the roads as they came by. The Dalmatian's job was to simply guard and navigate the horses that were pulling the carriages for the firefighters. There's a reason Marshall the firefighter pup from Paw Patrol is a Dalmatian! Dalmatians have a Pointer-like appearance, but of course they are best known for their spotty coats. If you want a dog that will be admired by people when you are out on a walk, the Dalmatian is an excellent choice! They came from Croatia in the Dalmatia region during the 16th century and it is believed that Pointers and Spotted Great Danes are ancestors. Dalmatians are also associated with an 'annual commemoration day' every year on the 1st of October known as National Fire

Pup Day. This is because the Dalmatian is the official mascot for the fire department. Without proper socialisation from an early age, Dalmatians can be skittish around strangers due to their guarding nature, but if you own horses the Dalmatian is sure to get along naturally with them as they are originally a carriage dog. Many floppy eared dog breeds are prone to ear infections and a significant percentage of Dalmatians can suffer deafness, so be sure to provide the best care for your spotty companion. The best activities for an athletic dog like the Dalmatian should be jogging or cycling together. You could also combine the land athletics with aquatics and do some water retrieving. To really simulate the Dalmatian's horse and carriage duties with the fire department, an obstacle course is the perfect activity.

THE FRENCH BULLDOG

Onto a smaller Utility Dog, the fun loving French Bulldog! The British Bulldog was bred out of Bull Baiting and into a companion dog in Britain during the 1800's. Some cross breeding with smaller terrier dogs and pugs began in order to create a smaller Bulldog as a companion. The new breed was taken to France with Nottingham lace-makers and officially named the French Bulldog! 'Frenchies' have become a popular dog breed for families with children from their affectionate demeanour. Similar to the British Bulldog, Frenchies are easy dogs to look after and always love to be with their loving owners! The French Bulldog is prone to Obstructed Airways Syndrome and must be monitored safely in hotter conditions. Frenchies may require more physical exercise than the British Bulldog, but there are many ways for a good owner to be creative when having fun. Ever wanted to play hide and seek with a dog? If you can teach your Frenchie a simple stay command whilst you hide, your dog will enjoy the task of searching around the house for its best friend-you! Almost like man-trailing. Taking a French Bulldog to the park and chasing a football or fetching a tennis ball can also be endless fun for both you and the dog. Another great activity for almost every dog would be a good puzzle like a snuffle mat.

THE SCHNAUZER TERRIER

The Schnauzer Terrier was originally bred in Berlin, Germany with an intelligent, comical and energetic personality. Though a Terrier breed, the Schnauzer was originally bred as a farm dog used not just to chase away vermin, but also herding livestock. Like many dogs, Schnauzer Terriers are devoted to their owners and will never want to be without them. While the Schnauzer is a highly intelligent dog making them easy to train, they are known for having the common Terrier trait of stubbornness. These breeds need attention and activity, otherwise they are quite prone to becoming bored which makes for a stubborn, irritable dog. To ease the stress and boredom of a Schnauzer Terrier, introduce obstacle courses or agility to feed the Schnauzer's physical needs along with retrieving activities. Schnauzers' love to use their brains and work out puzzles such as snuffle mats, proving how intelligent they are and how much they need mental stimulation for happiness. Although the Schnauzer is referred to as a terrier, it's actually recognised by the Kennel Club as a Utility Dog.

THE CHOW CHOW

Ever been unsure if you're more of a cat or dog person? The fluffy and cuddly Chow Chow might just be the happy medium you're looking for! Known as the 'bear dog', nobody can be too sure where the magnificent Chow Chow came from. However, it has been believed that the breed came from Mongolia, China thousands of years ago and possibly evolved from the ancient Tibetan Mastiff. Queen Victoria was said to be fond of the breed and may have instigated popularity for the Chow Chow. Chow Chows were originally used as hunting dogs in China as well as guard dogs and even used for pulling cargo from boats, similar to the Newfie. These days they are more of a companion dog like many of the Utility breeds. Chow Chows have a more catlike personality in that they are more independent than most dogs and might not always require the constant company of their owners. Maybe you or one of your friends occasionally enjoys some time alone, and the Chow Chow can sometimes be just the same. The Chow

Chow might be difficult to please, but that's not to say there are no fun activities for you the owner to provide them with. Mental stimulation from obedience training and correct socialisation are vital activities for Chow Chows. Because this breed is not always naturally outgoing and might not take to small children or other dogs, it's highly recommended to get them used to all kinds of different environments and different people at an early age. If your family take part in any hunting sports, then your Chow Chow will love taking part in some tracking and retrieving activities as it really simulates their early days in China. When you have trained and socialised the perfect Chow Chow, you and your dog may also enjoy putting everything to the test and enter dog shows together. In conclusion, Utility Dogs can all be perfect K9 companions, providing they get all their needs met with some considerate love and care. It's best to always research their history to understand what really makes them happy. However, these dogs are ideal for families due to their lenient nature.

QUIZ

Which dog is said to have been promoted by Queen Victoria?

Which dog has been made famous by a disney film?

Which dogs suffer from obstructed airways syndrome?

Chapter 5
Hounds

Hounds were bred to hunt mammals such as rabbits, foxes, badgers and deer. While hunting, the dogs in the Hound group are split into two teams. Sight Hounds are athletically built with long legs and superb vision for chasing prey, while Scent Hounds are more skilled in tracking down where their prey has been. They do this by using their nose before pursuing. Some dogs in the Hound group are known to be very vocal and will let out a long and loud howl. Because of this, you will always know where they are.

THE BEAGLE

A howling Hound with strong prey drive and intense vocalisation is the beloved Beagle. The Beagle is a very popular Hound to own and is everything you would want from a good hunting dog. Beagles have been used as hunting dogs from all the way back to Ancient Greece and although they are commonly owned as domestic pets, they are still determined hunters to this day. The Beagle was officially established in 15th century England and would be teamed up with hunters on horseback leading the way typically in pursuit of hares. The biggest trait known within the Beagle is its extremely loud vocals, which is ironic considering both 'Snoopy' (From Peanuts) and 'Gromit' (From Wallace and Gromit) are Beagles and yet they are silent. The howling unfortunately is one of the common reasons that Beagles get sent to shelters and re-homed. The howling can often come from boredom and a happy Beagle should be getting plenty of breed fulfilment. If your Beagle is stubborn with terrible recall due to the strong prey drive creating distractions, you can utilise the tracking skills and create a trail of tasty treats behind you everywhere you go. Beagles are very food driven and this can build some excellent engagement with your Beagle as they will follow you everywhere and not want to miss any food opportunities. Man-trailing could become an exciting game of hide and seek for you and your dog. A Beagle will find it incredibly rewarding to be given lots of praise and food after using the mighty nose to track down their best friend. And if that's not enough, snuffle mats are always going to keep a Beagle's nose and mind stimulated. Despite Beagle's being vocal little tykes, they are incredibly tame and content dogs that will add love and light to your life. They are fantastic around children, gentle in their pursuits and a furry friend you will find it hard to be without.

THE BLOODHOUND

A Hound that got its name from smelling the blood of a human is the stubborn yet affectionately noble BloodHound! The BloodHound is sadly on the verge of extinction, but has a long history of scent work, this is thanks to their gifted nose with a sense of smell said to be close to 1000 times more powerful than a human nose. BloodHounds came from Belgium & France originally tracking down foxes, deer and wild boar for hunters during the 14th century, and they have even been used to track down missing humans, getting their scent from any item of clothing belonging to the individual. Truly the ultimate man-hunter! The BloodHound has a remarkable talent for scent tracking utilised by man to hunt down criminals or missing loved ones. During the mid 17th century, BloodHounds were also used for tracking down victims of American slavery. This means that when dogs get breed fulfilment, they should use their magnificent powers for good and not evil. With great power comes great responsibility and it's the responsibility of you, the owner. Have no fear, there are some fantastic activities to give BloodHounds breed fulfilment. Though it would be morally wrong to go fox hunting nowadays, your BloodHound still needs breed fulfilment and one way you could replicate scent hunting is by getting the dog familiar with the scent of perhaps your hat or glove and then letting them track it down wherever you hide it. Sherlock Holmes's dog Toby would take immense pleasure tracking down anybody after sniffing something as simple as their hat and your BloodHound will love this game too! Another idea is to hide some food all around a room for your dog to then search. You can also hide some tasty treats under a cup and then mix it amongst other cups for your BloodHound to try and find it. Overall The BloodHound will love any game that involves using their nose, but try not to help them. The more challenging makes it all the more rewarding for a happy BloodHound.

THE BASSET HOUND

The short-legged elephant-eared Basset Hound is another Scent Hound known for being another dedicated tracker of scents, but also on the other hand, being very happy to sleep most of the day away. You truly get the best of both worlds with the Basset Hound. It is said to be believed that the Basset Hound was a result of a mutation in genes from the BloodHound, originally referring to the Basset Hound as a 'Dwarf Hound'. This new Hound breed was officially recognised in the 15th century but the Kennel Club hadn't registered the breed as the Basset Hound until the 19th century. Basset Hounds were popular hunting companions for French aristocrats and grew in popularity after the French Revolution. Apart from when they are hunting, Basset Hounds are not very energetic in the house making them perfect family pets if you have a busy lifestyle. Compared to other dogs, they are quite low-maintenance but still need adequate breed fulfilment. Basset Hounds have gentle and affectionate personalities and will typically get along nicely with humans and other dogs. The Basset Hound has a long and sad looking face, truly the Mona Lisa of the

K9 world. Basset Hounds are very happy dogs when given the appropriate breed fulfilment. Much like the BloodHound, Basset Hounds have a strong sense of smell and were bred with their short legs to keep their noses close to the ground when tracking. The long floppy ears also help stir up these scents towards the nose. It's no secret that like many dogs the Basset Hound can benefit so much from doing some scent work, puzzles like the good old snuffle mat will work perfectly for them. Although they are couch potatoes, Basset Hounds still need some exercise as they can easily become overweight. Taking your Basset Hound out exploring lots of new environments like towns, forests or even the seaside will give them lots of interesting new smells for them to take in. Much like the Beagle, Basset Hounds can be stubborn when it comes to recall as all the interesting scents can easily distract them, so be sure to build a strong bond. Tug of war is a nice and simple game for you and your Basset Hound to play together without having to mobilise too much. If you let them win each time, your Basset Hound is certain to want to play with you again and again!

THE DACHSHUND

Over to the smallest and possibly the most adorable little Hound, known as the 'sausage dog' is the glorious Dachshund! This fascinating sausage-bodied pup is today seen as more of a toy dog, but the Dachshund is still a Hound and has its genetic hunting instincts. Dachshunds were bred and Kennel Club registered in 15th Century Germany to hunt badgers from their dens. "Dachs" means badger and "Hund" means dog, thus we get the name Dachshund! Dachshunds would also hunt in packs to hunt larger animals like deer and wild boar, mostly tracking prey as they are Scent Hounds. These days Dachshunds get immense luxury living as family pets and are loyal and affectionate to their owners, however they may dig up your back garden thinking it might be a badger's den. This happens when your Dachshund is bored and longing for breed fulfilment. These days, Dachshunds are 'fashionable' pets that are purchased without thinking about their inner needs. They become very docile, yet naturally lively little things. They need correct breed fulfilment just like bigger dogs, even though their smaller size might make them seem otherwise. In addition to using a snuffle mat when your Dachshund is in the comfort of your home, find a quiet open spot when the two of you are out on a walk and hide some tasty treats in the grass, then let the dog sniff and search for them. It's a very simple and relaxed way to let Dachshunds use their natural sniffing abilities. They may be only little Hounds, but Dachshunds must stay reasonably active or else they can gain weight because of their long torso above their short stubby legs. As a result they are prone to developing intervertebral disc disease. This is a disease whereby the discs that separate the spine breakdown, separating the bones in the spine and causing pain in the back and neck. To avoid this, keep them as active as possible. You can enjoy a fun game of fetch with a ball or even using toys for chasing like an RC car, any thrilling activity to get your Dachshund moving and tapping into their hunting instincts, but always let them capture the toy after chasing. Similar to Terriers, Dachshunds also love to dig and this can be done in the appropriate environments such as the seaside or out in the woods or maybe even treat them to a sandpit in your back garden.

THE RHODESIAN RIDGEBACK

Originating in the picturesque coastal world of South Africa is the magnificent Rhodesian Ridgeback! 'Ridgies' are incredibly heroic Hounds with a strong drive to protect and please their owners. They display a similar physical appearance to the Labrador Retriever in a fox-red colour coat. Ridgies are very sociable dogs that very much prefer the constant company of other dogs in their pack or human family members, this is most likely because back in the 1800's they would typically hunt in packs and required a large amount of teamwork with whatever task they were undertaking, be it tracking down the scent of prey or defending their loving owners from Lions. The Rhodesian Ridgeback is also known as the Lion Hound as these fearless dogs are most famous for taking on lions in the ring if their owners were ever in danger. Over the years Ridgies have become more mellow and will happily sleep most of the day as a domestic pet in a cosy house. With that said, they still can become bored and destructive like all dogs when they are not given enough stimulation in their life. Being outdoorsy dogs, Ridgies are keen to explore all kinds of different environments especially with their loving owners on a walk. If you are a competitive dog owner, an excellent bonding experience for both you and your Ridgie would be to enter dog shows and demonstrate training tricks. A good old game of fetch can be taken to the next level by introducing impulse control, making your dog wait before they retrieve. This teaches them that all the good stuff will come to them whenever they are calm and relaxed.

THE GREYHOUND

The Greyhound is not only one of the most popular Hound dogs to own as a family pet, but also one of the fastest Sight Hounds on the planet. Truly the Formula 1 racing car of the K9 world. Although they might appear underweight, Greyhounds are pure muscle with an aerodynamic and athletic build for speed and determination. This breed can be traced back thousands of years ago to ancient Egypt and then growing in popularity in both Greece and Rome. Greyhounds were used to pursue other speedy mammals like deer and hare, running up to 45 miles per hour. By the 20th century after increasing popularity within European royalty, the Greyhound took part in modern dog racing sports with the use of mechanical hares to lure them along the track. This sport has continued over the years to the present date. Contrary to popular belief, Greyhounds are naturally couch potatoes like Basset Hounds. They certainly have their energy and speed when they need it, but would happily spend most of the day relaxing in a comfy bed at home, making Greyhounds suitable dogs for busy households. Many Greyhounds can be found in shelters after they retire from racing typically at the age of 5 or 6 years old. Their dream retirement home is with a loving family like yours, but don't forget to give them plenty of mental stimulation for when they are not snoozing. A Greyhound will get lots of excitement chasing an RC car to replicate their origins pursuing fast hares. You could build an obstacle course and make all the running around slightly more challenging for your Greyhound, this could then lead to agility too. Though they are not traditionally a retrieving dog, some Greyhounds actually do enjoy chasing a ball to bring back to their best friend. This could be you!

THE BORZOI

One of the most intelligent yet stubborn Sight Hounds is the Borzoi, also known as the Russian Wolfhound! Like the Greyhound, the Borzoi is another speedy Hound bred for hunting deer, rabbits and hare. The Borzoi originally came from 17th Century Russia and would accompany hunters on horseback. The Borzoi got its name from a Russian term that simply means "fast". Borzois are calm and affectionate towards their owners with an independent quality that you can find in cats. Borzois prefer families that are calm and relaxed more so than younger children or smaller pets like rabbits and guinea pigs . Similar to the Greyhound, Borzois are happy to snooze throughout some of the day, but can also get bored and still require activities to liven things up. If you are a horse rider, your Borzoi may enjoy the fresh air and trot along beside you and your horse. Agility is a fun running sport that Borzois can excel in as long as you give them very patient training, the same can be said when entering dog shows. A Sight

Hound sporting event called Lure Coursing involves running along an appropriate track with a mechanical line like a fishing rod attached to a toy or empty bag as bait to chase. This sport very much simulates both the Borzoi and Greyhound's original job to chase rabbits and they enjoy it very much.

THE SALUKI

One of the most ancient Sight Hounds in addition to the Greyhound and Borzoi is the very graceful Saluki. It is believed that the Saluki as a breed has been around for thousands of years originally from various parts of the world such as Egypt, Greece and the Middle-east. You can find many ancient paintings of Salukis hunting in the deserts alongside Nomadic tribes on horseback. It wasn't until the 1920's when the American kennel club officially registered the Saluki as a breed. Like many Sight Hounds, the Saluki has a tremendous ability to run fast at a speed up to 50 miles per hour in pursuit of typically hare, fox and gazelle. They also possess impeccable eye vision to monitor their prey. Did you know that the Saluki is the royal dog of Egypt? Many Pharaohs kept Salukis and many Arabians declared the breed "a noble gift from god". This was to compliment their ability to work hard and endure the hot temperatures and maintain a lot of energy. Very much like the Borzoi, Salukis have a cat-like independent nature that can make training challenging, they need patience and perseverance from their owners. Athletes like the Saluki really need enough physical and mental stimulation to avoid behavioural issues. Even though Salukis are Sight Hounds, they do enjoy tracking and doing scent work. This is a golden opportunity for the two of you to develop engagement and a strong bond together. Because Salukis are independent and love to run around, letting them off the lead could be a challenge if you are not in a secure environment. Teach your Saluki a cue for eye contact and constantly reward them with a tasty treat every time they look at you, even without being asked to. Once you've made yourself more interesting to your Saluki than any distractions, and you become inseparable, why not take part in dog shows or even sports like agility? The perfect owner for a Saluki is someone who loves to run just as much as they do. Go for a jog or cycle together in the fresh air and blue skies. If you have a keen interest in charity and fundraising, you and your Saluki could make such a perfect team and run a race or obstacle course together to raise money for a good cause.

THE IRISH WOLFHOUND

The gigantic and majestic Sight Hound that is the Irish WolfHound originated in the rural countryside of Donegal, Ireland. This wolf-like pooch worked in packs during the late 1800s to hunt wolves and they certainly look the part. The Irish WolfHound was an extremely desirable breed to own and became popular in European and Celtic royal families, using them for hunting wolves and even bears, much like the Medieval Scottish DeerHounds that appear in the Pixar movie "Brave" to hunt down a bear. Standing up to around 3 feet tall and weighing up to 80 kg, Irish WolfHounds are not best suited to a home with valuables. The modern evolved Irish WolfHound we know today is actually a recreation of the original breed and is much bigger today than back then. British Army Office and dog breed Captain George Augustus Graham revived the breed by gathering breeds such as the Scottish DeerHound, the Tibetan Mastiff, the Great Dane and a Borzoi belonging to the then Duchess of Newcastle, Kathleen

Pelham-Clinton. The modern Irish WolfHound nowadays has a more sweet and gentle personality compared to the hunting dog it used to be, this could be a genetic trait from its ancestor the Great Dane. The energy needs of a modern Irish WolfHound is not as high maintenance as you might think. They are as fast as Sight Hounds can be, running 30-40 miles per hour and yet they are happy to relax for most of the day just like the Greyhound. The Irish WolfHound is among the friendliest and most patient dogs that are eager to please their owners, making them a good choice for families. Some of the easiest breed fulfilment activities are perfect for an Irish WolfHound, such as tug of war. A game of tug of war every now and then is simple and can last as long or as short as you choose and they will always be up for a game if you let them win every time. Irish WolfHounds are still Sight Hounds, so they will always be content if you give them a ball to fetch or toy to chase. When socialised nicely with other dogs, they will enjoy chasing each other out in the wide open spaces and fresh air. Whenever you are out on a walk with your Irish WolfHound, find somewhere to sit down together and simply do nothing. As long as they are with you, they are at peace with the world.

THE WHIPPET

Is the Irish WolfHound maybe too big for your house? Ever wanted to own a racehorse and keep it in your home? Why not consider the smallest SightHound? The adorable Whippet. Compared to many ancient dogs, the Whippet is actually a relatively newer breed of dog. Bred in northern England in the late 18th century, the Whippet is a small Sight Hound with the Greyhound and smaller Terriers as ancestors. Whippets were popular to own within the working class and were bred to take on Terrier pest control duties and chase rabbits away on farms. Whippets were known as the Rabbit Hound for a while in their early days before their kennel club registration as the Whippet, which came from an old English term "Whappet " meaning small yelping dog. Known at the time as the poor man's racehorse, Whippet racing became a popular sport replicating the Greyhound races. Whippets can run up to 35 - 40 miles per hour thanks to their double suspension gallop in which all four legs come off the ground both extended and tucked in as they run along the track. In recent years, Whippets have even worked as therapy dogs and provide emotional support to their owners. Whippets are devoted to their families and get along nicely with children and other dogs, however they are wary of strangers and can be sensitive to any abnormalities. The best activities for a Whippet can be as basic as chasing a football or fetching a ball, but Lure Coursing is one of their favourite sports in addition to agility. Whippets love nothing more than taking on the challenge of chasing bait on a string while avoiding obstacles along the way. Flyball is another thrilling dog sport for many Pastoral Dogs and Terriers, but that's not to say a Whippet can't participate. Flyball is a dog relay sport and involves dogs jumping over hurdles from one side of the room to the other. At each side there is a contraption that releases a ball as fast as lightning for the dog to chase and retrieve. Flyball can even be done at home with two people standing at each side of the garden to throw a ball. In conclusion, Hounds have a mix of personalities and talents involving scent work, athleticism and sometimes a mix of the two. Much like families, they come in different sizes and styles. Be sure to choose a Hound that integrates perfectly with your family and lifestyle.

QUIZ

Which Hound belongs to famous dogs, Snoopy and Gromit?

Which Hound got their name from the blood of humans?

Which Hound is also known as the 'Russian WolfHound?'

Pastoral Dogs have the job of moving livestock around from fields to trailers where they can be moved into barns for shelter. The livestock can include sheep, various cattle and even reindeer. Pastoral Dogs are highly intelligent, energetic and trainable. This allows them to pay close attention to what their owners are asking them to do and learn very quickly how to achieve their tasks.

All Pastoral Dogs are bred and trained to be hyper-vigilant, always diligent in the protection of their livestock. Every dog needs breed fulfillment, but if there was just one breed group that needed a job more than the others, it would be the Pastoral group. The Pastoral group are hard-working, evolving and adapting.

THE BORDER COLLIE

A very intelligent, athletic and even acrobatic Pastoral Dog is the classic and glorious sheepdog known as the Border Collie.

Getting its name from its origin along the English Scottish border, the Border Collie has proven since the 1700s to be a very useful dog to herd livestock. So much so that the word "Collie" comes from an old Celtic term for 'useful'.

The very first and famous Border Collie was known as 'Old Hemp' and was the 'stud' dog that evolved the modern Border Collie that we all know and love today.

Old Hemp was born in Northumberland, England in the September of 1893 and lived to the age of 7 when he sadly passed away in the May of 1901. Old Hemp fathered over 200 puppies in his lifetime. He demonstrated a quiet and less aggressive attitude towards his herding work and this characteristic has been passed down through generations of Border Collies today.

Border Collies have been clever enough to read their owners like a book, often able to predict what they are about to ask before they are given the command. If they are not trained properly from a young age, Border Collies can become very nervous and even shy. This is because they really want to please their owners and without any training they can struggle to figure out their tasks and their nerves get the better of them. The nervousness can lead to behavioural problems such as excessive barking, digging and even trying to herd children around the house.

Breed fulfilment is the solution to prevent many unwanted behaviours. Border Collies love herding activities which is perfect if you own any livestock for them to herd. They have a unique way of keeping their bodies low to the ground while moving around fast on their feet, they almost slither around and prowl like a cat.

Border Collies are similar to the kids in school who love to learn and get immense satisfaction from gaining new skills. Training a Border Collie at an early age is imperative. Fortunately because they are considered to be the smartest dogs in the world, Border Collies are very easy to train, they learn very quickly and are always eager to learn more tricks. The list is endless when it comes to all the cool tricks you can teach your Border Collie, there's a reason most of the performing dogs on TV show *'Britain's Got Talent'* are Border Collies.

Agility is a sport that many dogs can benefit from, but the Border Collie is hands down the ultimate pro when it comes to agility. Not only is the Border Collie brilliant at agility, but they are also champions at Flyball. Both the sports require dogs to complete an obstacle course against the clock and the Border Collie is always trying to beat their own record. The ultimate self-motivated goal chaser.

Simple games of fetch or dock diving to retrieve in water will keep a Border Collie reasonably happy, but if you, the owner, think they've had enough you're wrong! They will want to keep going all day long. It's important to preserve their joints and not excessively burn them out when retrieving, but you will have to be the one who ends the game.

Once your Border Collie has received their daily breed fulfilling activities, you should motivate them to have a rest and give them a long lasting chew to unwind and relax with.

THE ROUGH COLLIE

Over to one of the most elegant and heroic looking Pastoral Dogs, the Rough Collie. Your parents may recognise this breed from the iconic film, *Lassie* where the famous line "Lassie, come home!" originated from.

The breed itself Originated in Scotland in 1860. Rough Collies are large, graceful dogs known for their long and rough double coats to protect them in snowy weather.

Peter Rabbit author, Beatrix Potter had a pet Rough Collie named Kep, who was featured as a character in many of her stories.

As far as Pastoral Dogs go, the Rough Collie is very gentle natured and works well herding livestock, but can also have an off switch after a hard day's work and then relax with their families at home. Like many Pastoral Dog breeds, Rough Collies can develop unwanted behaviours if they are bored and not given enough training and stimulation. These behaviours are usually barking and destructive bursts of energy. However, by appropriate training and activities, you can prevent this negative behaviour becoming second nature.

Rough Collies are not naturally guard dogs, however they will bark at strangers passing by to alert their owners of any suspicious activity. Along with the Border Collie, Rough Collies are very easy to train and they are ranked among the most intelligent dog breeds in the world. They love to learn new tricks!

Rough Collies have even been used as therapy dogs to provide companionship and emotional support for their owners. Though typically the work of the Labrador or Golden Retriever, Rough Collies also utilise their intelligence and work well as guide dogs for the blind.

It's worth mentioning before considering a Rough Collie, that the price of owning a Rough Collie can be extortionate with food, vet and grooming bills combined together. So before making this decision, make sure this is something plausible for your family.

When it comes to breed fulfilling activities for a Rough Collie, there is always agility and herding activities that come very natural to them. Teaching new tricks will always tire out a Rough Collie mentally and create a very strong bond with their owners. Some Rough Collies enjoy retrieving which you could then advance to teaching a place command. This would really come in handy to teach them how to put their own toys away.

Treibball is an excellent outlet for Pastoral Dogs with no access to any livestock. This involves all the voice and hand commands for herding sheep, only this time the dog is moving a large bouncy ball instead! Your dog will certainly get the same excitement of herding whilst challenging their bodies and their minds.

THE SAMOYED

One of the fluffiest Pastoral dogs on the planet is the magnificent polar bear-like Samoyed! Similar to the Siberian Husky, the Samoyed gets its name from the Samoyedic people of Siberia who assisted with pulling sleds when traveling as well as taking on the task of herding reindeer. Samoyeds are known for their white fluffy double coats. They can be spotted from a mile away by their luxurious looking coats. It has been believed that Samoyeds originally were black and brown, but the colour was bred out of them into the white colour we know them to have. This was to protect them by reflecting in the sunlight to keep them cool and prevent them from overheating when they worked. Unless you and your Samoyed reside in snowy mountains, an excellent form of breed fulfillment is to do some retrieving activities with agility combined. This will simulate their jobs of running and moving fast while avoiding obstacles in their way. And if it's not the physical activities that make Samoyeds happy, a good snuffle mat will certainly keep their minds busy like many dogs.

THE GERMAN SHEPHERD

If you and your family have been thinking about taking on a more challenging dog breed where you can provide very versatile training techniques, the German Shepherd may be the way to go. Although they require more high maintenance training techniques, they will reward you by being protective and keeping you safe.

The German Shepherd has been a very popular Pastoral Dog to own ever since its origins in late 1890s Germany. The German Shepherd was bred to herd and protect livestock as well as assisting humans for many different purposes. German Shepherds are very powerful and intelligent dogs, making them incredibly trainable in the right hands. The German Shepherd is often considered to be more of a working breed. This is because they have many skills on their CV such as search and rescue work with the police force and guiding/assisting the blind.

Because they are vocal and natural guard dogs, German Shepherds are also used for attacking criminals due to their killer instincts when it comes to providing protection. You truly must ask yourself whether you are the sort of person that can rise to the challenge of training such a loyal yet naturally confrontational guarding breed. Many German Shepherds are re-homed as a result of no research or preparation from the owners. But that's what this book is all about.

The key to preventing any behaviour difficulties that can come with a German Shepherd is to make sure you train them correctly from day 1 as a puppy and provide them with fulfilling outlets. This will make your German Shepherd the devoted loving best friend you have been dreaming of.

Did you know that dogs such as spaniels and retrievers come in two types? There is a working line that's more athletic and energetic for working, and then there is a show line which is more solid in build and less energetic making them more suited as a family pet. German Shepherds are exactly the same and a show line German Shepherd is going to display slightly less energy, softer and easier to keep as a pet, but still a dog that requires stimulation in their life.

It is highly recommended that you socialise a German Shepherd to various different environments, sounds, people and other animals. If in doubt, get a professional behaviourist to steer you in the right direction. Seeking help out of love for your pet is sometimes the right way to go.

Taking a German Shepherd on some exciting hikes is perfect for physical fitness, but why not stop somewhere and play training games together like retrieving on your command? A German

Shepherd with stupendous impulse control will always come in handy in many situations. Combine fetch with dock diving, getting your dog to jump in water and swim out to retrieve for its loving leader.

Agility is always going to be excellent for simulating police work or herding livestock. If your dog excels in the sport, you may wish to compete in dog shows together.

At home you and your German Shepherd can enjoy a simple game of tug of war and build a strong bond together. This gives you a dog that always wants to engage and play with you.

THE BELGIAN MALINOIS

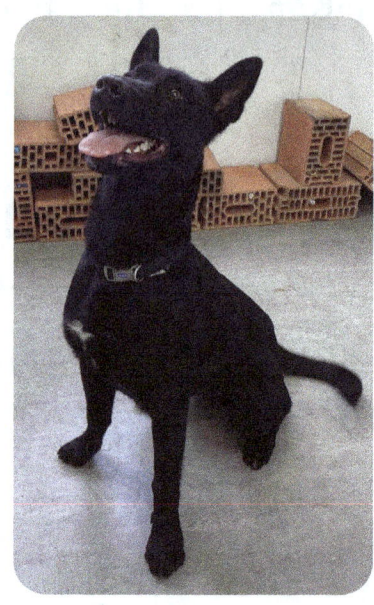

While German Shepherds are best suited with highly skilled and experienced owners, the Belgian Malinois is on the next level up!

Owning a 'Mali' requires lots of skill and training, they can become aggressive when in the wrong hands. Professional behaviourist training is vital. They are extremely alert and highly intelligent for their own good. Malis are not traditionally recommended for owners who want a simple domestic pet, as they are bred with a killer instinct for police work, search and rescue missions, herding and guarding sheep. Belgian Malinois are the most fearless, hard working breed of dog there has ever been. They are loyal to their owners and will go through anything to protect them from danger.

The Belgian Malinois originated in Belgium during the 1880s as a shepherd breed in the city of Mechelen which is where the name Malinois came from. Malis are very agile and acrobatic dogs which makes them very useful if the police ever need them to jump high or even climb their way in pursuit of criminals. Like many Pastoral Dog breeds, Malis are incredibly focused and eager to please their owners. There are lots of Malis around the world working in the police to detect illegal substances and stolen goods, as well as searching for people who are missing.

The personality of a Belgian Malinois is very much workaholic, whether it be law enforcement, herding, guarding and even assisting disabled people. Malis are incredibly employable dogs. They are also one of the healthiest dogs in the world, which benefits everything they endure within police and military operations.

Soldiers who worked with these incredible dogs sometimes had to do a tandem jump from an aeroplane, while attached to their four legged companions!

You may not wish to own a Mali right now, but maybe someday you want to work in the police or military when you grow up. This is a good starting point for researching Malis. Although Belgian Malinois are not usually pet dogs, there are still some who need a home. It is unlikely, but on the chance they fail their police or military training, they are left to be adopted. These animals need love like any other.

The best activities for Malis can include various sports like flyball and agility, anything that involves intense physical and mental stimulation.

Malis are devoted to their owners making them prone to being overprotective. Socialising them from day 1 to various other people and dogs in a variety of environments is a priority with the support of a professional trainer. The simple way to achieve this is by taking them out to different places and applying lots of rewarding and positive reinforcement. That way the dog will enjoy the experience and look forward to doing it again.

Man-trailing is the perfect way to replicate the search and rescue missions a Mali will do in the police and military.

Dogs as highly intelligent as a Belgian Malinois will benefit so much from doing lots of problem solving. Snuffle mats are great for this, but you can make it even more challenging by putting lots of tasty treats in a plastic bottle and letting the dog get them out. It keeps them very busy.

THE OLD ENGLISH SHEEPDOG

One of the largest and shaggiest Pastoral Dogs known for being the official mascot for *Dulux Paint* is the big cuddly teddy bear-esque Old English Sheepdog!

Old English Sheepdogs do not have a clear origin. Many believe that they originated from southwestern England in the early 19th century with the Bearded Collie and Russian Owtchar as possible ancestors. The name Old English Sheepdog remains a bit of a mystery, they are a relatively new breed with possible Russian ancestry making them not fully English and they are not often used as sheepdogs. Isn't that peculiar?

The only herding link to Old English Sheepdogs is that they were used to drive livestock along the roads towards markets.

These big fluffy doggies can weigh up to 45kg and require regular haircuts for their thick, fluffy double coats. Old English Sheepdogs are a large breed that may not finish growing and filling out until they are approximately one year old. It's important to bear their physical appearance in mind for your family home and valuable items.

Similar to the Boxer, Old English Sheepdogs have a very playful and goofy personality, so it's important to apply a lot of patience when training. Old English Sheepdogs are very good natured and fairly adaptable for various lifestyles, making them good family pets. They don't actually require much breed fulfilment to be happy dogs. They just want to be with their loving families and get fuss and attention all day long!

The perfect owner for an Old English Sheepdog is someone who has a great sense of humour when it comes to their clownish nature and doesn't mind the high maintenance of grooming their double coats. It is also recommended they can provide enough space for such a large and bouncy dog!

When it comes to breed fulfilling an Old English Sheepdog, the basics of playing fetch and tug of war will keep them content. They enjoy puzzles like snuffle mats and searching for any food you hide for them in long grass or around the house.

THE AUSTRALIAN SHEPHERD

Australian Shepherds are another intellectual Pastoral Dog breed with such affection for their family. Australian Shepherds were actually bred in the western United States of America during the 1800s to herd the livestock of ranchers, cowboys and farmers. However it has been believed that ancestor Collies for this breed did come over from Australia which is why they are called Australian Shepherds.

'Aussies' have the typical Pastoral Dog personalities of being athletic, hard working and always eager to please. They are fast learners making them very easily trained, but they also have a playful side to them. They work hard and they also know how to have fun. Aussies will warm to strangers, but might be a little protective at first. It's very natural for them to be worried about their families, however this can be prevented with appropriate socialising when they are young puppies.

Aussies are impeccable at managing all kinds of jobs from obviously herding, but also in scent work for search and rescue operations and even assisting the disabled with emotional and physical support. Aussies love to help people reach down for slippers or books or magazines if needed. They're such thoughtful friends.

Australian Shepherds are happy to try anything, which is great because this means you can explore all kinds of different ways to give your dog breed fulfilment. Aussies enjoy both agility and flyball with lots of running around and jumping hurdles along the way. Playing fetch on both land and in water will always keep them happy.

Australian Shepherds are interesting members of the Pastoral Dogs team as they have a very strong sense of smell, this can be put to the test by signing up for man-trailing classes. Your Aussie will definitely want to rise to the challenge of using their nose and searching for someone they love very much. This could be you!

THE PEMBROKE WELSH CORGI

Now here's a slightly smaller Pastoral Dog with such a cute recognisable appearance, the Pembroke Welsh Corgi.

Originally bred in Pembroke, Wales and can be traced way back to the 10th century. The development of this breed remains unclear, however researchers believe that the Corgi may have evolved from various cattle dog breeds from vikings that were brought over to reside in Wales. Corgis worked herding various cattle and proved themselves very capable by being smaller and agile dogs.

Much like the Basset Hound nicknamed as a 'dwarf-dog', Corgis display a similar appearance with their short legs. Their name "Corgi" is simply a Welsh translation for "Dwarf Dog". Though Corgis are known for their friendly and playful personalities, Corgis are another Pastoral Dog that can be wary of strangers. Both the Corgi and Rough Collie are naturally watch dogs, very vocal when it comes to protecting their owner's property.

The Corgi is considered to be the royal dog - Queen Elizabeth II was given Corgis as pets by her father King George the 6th and she owned over 30 Corgis! To this day, many associate Corgi's with our late Queen mother to King Charles.

It's safe to say Corgis have been a popular breed of dog for centuries now, but what activities are best for you and your Corgi? Fetching and retrieving will be simple and fun for your Corgi and with some impulse control thrown in, you will have an excitable but also obedient dog waiting to fetch once you give them the command.

Corgis enjoy scent work such as finding their favourite treats hidden in the grassy fields or maybe snuffle mats if it's raining outside.

They may be small, but Corgis enjoy obstacle courses like agility which will feed their herding instincts nicely. If you want to do some herding training with your Corgi but don't own any livestock, your Corgi will have endless fun rolling a large ball around to simulate herding.

Now that you know about Pastoral Dogs, you will know they are very loyal, smart and energetic dogs with strong herding instincts that always love to learn new tricks. They long for work in whatever capacity, so be sure to give them an outlet to make them feel really useful and happy dogs. If you think this is the dog for you, you're in for a treat. No dog is as protective, loyal and ambitious as the Pastoral Dogs.

QUIZ

Which part of England did old Hemp come from?

Which Pastoral Dog was owned by Beatrix Potter?

Which Pastoral Dog can sky dive?

Toy dogs are very small breeds of dogs. Though they are tiny and almost 'pocket-sized', their size is overtaken by their many different personalities. The best thing about Toy Dogs is that apart from all being small lap dogs to cuddle up with, they can still be different to each other. This breed category is full of various personalities and interesting backgrounds. They are mainly companion dogs and display the same loyalty and devotion you get from dogs in the Working group. It's their job to be your companion after all!

THE CAVALIER KING CHARLES SPANIEL

Ranked among the top ten most popular dogs to own is the sweet, versatile and adorable Cavalier King Charles Spaniel. Despite being a Spaniel breed, 'Cavys' are not the same Gun Dog as Cocker and Springer Spaniels. Despite this, they share similarities in personality with a less work driven temperament. Cavys coexist well with humans of all ages and other animals, rarely showing any signs of aggression. Bred in England during the early 1900s, the Cavalier King Charles Spaniel was bred to be a companion dog to accompany the upper class on request in various public places. They even slept in beds with their owners to keep them warm when suffering from sickness. They were named after 'King Charles the 2nd' who took a shine to them. When it comes to owning a Cavy, they are very easy to train and extremely sweet natured. Socialising comes naturally to Cavys, they will be your best friend in no time! The perfect home for a Cavalier King Charles Spaniel doesn't need to be specifically large or small, they are easily satisfied and will be just grateful to have a loving family. The Cavalier King Charles Spaniel may only be bred to be a lap dog, but they still need fun activities to prevent boredom. They might not take to agility like other spaniels, but Cavys love running and this is something you can easily do together in your back garden or out on walks. Cavys are very intelligent and easy to train. An idea could be to demonstrate your favourite tricks at dog shows. This will be fun and rewarding for you and your dog! Snuffle mats and various other scent puzzles are also great for Cavys, they're not quite hunting dogs, but they still have the incredible Spaniel nose to exercise.

THE POMERANIAN

Although they are known for being adorable little fluff balls, there are so many interesting qualities about the Pomeranian that make them excellent little companions for any sized family. Pomeranians were bred in Pomerania, Northern Europe in the 1700s as hunting dogs for smaller prey such as small birds and rodents. This made them evolve into naturally vocal dogs. They then grew in popularity among aristocrats and even royalty and retired from hunting to be companion dogs. Queen Victoria was very fond of dogs and owned many different breeds, the Pomeranian being one of them. The Pomeranian is a very small dog and stands at 7 inches, this means that they can very easily travel with you and your family on holidays. Pomeranians are happy in a giant palace or in a small house, they don't need loads of space to be happy. They need exercise on walks like all dogs and there are lots of fun activities to do with your Pomeranian that will help prevent boredom. These activities can include the classic snuffle mat or even hiding treats around the house to let your Pomeranian search for them. You could also tap into the Pomeranian's hunting instincts and prey drive by getting them to chase yourself or maybe a fast toy like an RC car.

THE MALTESE

Not only said to be the oldest Toy Dog breed, but also one of the oldest breed dating all the way back to 6000 BC according to Charles Darwin. There is no evidence to support the many theories of where the Maltese originated from. Some believe they came from a town in Sicily and some believe in Egypt, however there is some evidence of the roman governors in Malta owning the breed. This leads back to the Emperor Claudius bringing them to Britain. Malta would explain the breed name Maltese. These dogs were sold by traders to many royals and national leaders over the centuries as companion dogs. The Maltese is known for it's elegant snowy white coats which require lots of grooming maintenance and regular haircuts. They are energetic and full of character making them fun for your whole family to enjoy! First time dog owners will find the Maltese fairly easy to train as they are super intelligent and learn to please their owners quickly. It's highly recommended that you socialise your Maltese to lots of different environments, people and dogs as they can be snappy when not given proper training. Fun activities for your Maltese to enjoy can be retrieving on both land and water, burning off their energy with something fun like swimming after a ball. Tug of war is a great way to invite your Maltese to play a game with you and build lots of engagement. The Maltese displays a very strong sense of smell which can be put to the test when you hide their favourite treats in the grass or around the house for them to sniff and search. Leaving a trail of treats behind you on a walk will definitely bring you and your Maltese closer as they will never want to miss any food opportunities.

THE CHIHUAHUA

A dog that will make you think of reality stars hiding them in their handbags is the humble little Chihuahua. Many believe that the Chihuahua was the sacred companion to the Aztecs, residing in Mexican temples where they would witness rituals. It wasn't until the 1850s when the Chihuahua was officially named after the Mexican city of the same name. Chihuahuas were bred to help heal sickness by cuddling up to their owners to keep them warm, like a living hot water bottle. Chihuahuas are the smallest dog breeds in the world only standing up to 5 inches tall, this makes them very easy dogs to take to all kinds of environments when socialising. Lots of Chihuahuas have even enjoyed riding around in handbags as a result of their size. These dogs may be small, but they are alert and lively! Very similar to the Jack Russell Terrier or the Yorkshire Terrier. Chihuahuas are known as velcro dogs meaning they have one particular family member they always want to be with. This can result to some over protective measures taken on by the dog when strangers come to visit. The Chihuahua may be your best friend, but it helps to share responsibilities around the family and make sure they don't get too clingy with just one person. Chihuahua's are known for being vocal and playful, so if you are part of a family that enjoys more of a peaceful, calm environment they may not be for you. But that doesn't mean you can't appreciate their breed for what it is from afar. Chihuahuas are not great with young children, they can feel skittish around people with a similar amount of energy to themselves. It's best to carefully select the appropriate games to play together and create the best bonding experience. Do you like blowing bubbles? Well Chihuahuas love to chase bubbles! This can be a great way to burn off some energy for your dog and you will get immense satisfaction as you watch your best friend having lots of fun. Tug of war and fetch are both simple games that will allow your Chihuahua to not only have a good run around, but also interact with you! You can even fit some playtime in the middle of your walks. Training and teaching your Chihuahua lots of tricks will be rewarding for you as the trainer and for your dog who is always eager to please the loving leader.

THE PUG

While the Boxer is known as the clown of the K9 world, you might be looking for a smaller version. This small package comes in the form of a pug. The Pug we know today is a small 'cheeky chappie' type with a distinctive look and mischievous disposition. Although this is how we see them now, their origin is much different and on the contrast. Pugs originated from China as far back as 206-BC, many years later Pugs gained the common Toy Dog position as companions for royalty and the Chinese upper classes. Pugs lived luxuriously with Chinese Emperors all the way through to the early 1600s when they were brought to Europe through dog breed trading. Did you know that a famous British artist named William Hogarth was very fond of the Pug and would often include them in many of his paintings? This can verify their European existence as far back as the late 1600s and early 1700s. Some research suggests that Pugs were named after small monkeys in the South American rainforests that shared similar characteristics and physical features. Though other people believe that the name Pug evolved from a William Shakespeare character named Puck, a mischievous sprite in the infamous play 'A Midsummer Night's Dream'. As a consequence of Pugs being such ancient dogs, they have a flat nose and unique facial structure compared to other dogs, making them struggle to take long and deep breaths. Pugs suffer with obstruction in their airways and they struggle breathing even more when it's hot outside. If you own a Pug it's recommended that you keep them cool and don't let them run around too much, they will need to catch their breath. Much like the Boxer, Pugs require a lot of patience and a good sense of humour when training, but if you are diligent and consistent, your Pug will be the affectionate companion you always wanted. When it comes to giving your Pug fun activities to relieve stress and boredom, it's extremely important to remember they need regular rest breaks to catch their breath. In fact when you are taking a gentle walk in the park with your Pug, have a rest break on a bench or somewhere comfortable to relax. A great way to keep a Pug cool in the heat is swimming, but they will still need to take breaks. In that case, just let them paddle somewhere shallow or even treat them to a paddling pool in the back garden. You and your Pug could enjoy a very gentle game of fetch in the comfort of your home. Although, it is encouraged to only play for a couple of retrieves at a time for the benefit of the breed. A perfect game for a pug would be a puzzle toy to stimulate their minds without exhausting themselves from intense physical activity. Snuffle mats and many other treat dispensing toys will also do the job just fine.

THE SHIH TZU

Disclaimer for reader: If you are reading this book out loud, just remind your family that you are reading about dogs, now where were we? Shih Tzus are pint sized pups with so much love for their owners. This comes from once again being a popular ancient companion to Chinese royalty. A common theme amongst the Toy Dog breeds. The name Shih Tzu is a Mandarin term for "Little Lion". Research in China discovered ancient dog bones confirming the Shih Tzu's existence as far back as 8000-BC! That is one historical breed. Other research suggests that Shih Tzus were bred by Tibetan monks and given to royalty as gifts. As you can see, these adorable little dogs are rich with history and culture despite them being commonly known today as small, little dogs. The Shih Tzu is the epitome of what we want from a Toy Dog, to simply be a companion. Did you know that the Shih Tzu has been a companion for many famous people? Beyoncé, Mariah Carey, Paul O'Grady and even Queen Elizabeth II. Shih Tzus love playing with their owners and some of the best activities can involve retrieving as well as problem solving through puzzles like the always useful snuffle mat. This can be said for all dogs, but socialising can be really beneficial in the long run and with that in mind, your Shih Tzu will really enjoy a long run with other four legged friends on walks.

In conclusion, Toy Dogs are small, moderately energetic K9 companions who love to be treated like royalty and only want to be our best friends.They don't take up too much space and enjoy some of the easiest breed fulfilling activities. Overall their happy place is sleeping peacefully on your lap. Despite them being known as Toy Dogs, they have as many needs as bigger dogs and so when choosing your breed, you need to be sure you have a lot to offer these little packages with big hearts.

QUIZ

Which breeds descended from China?

Which breed is named after Monkeys from SA rainforests?

Which breed was bred in England in the early 1900s?

Which breed is not suitable for young children?

Chapter 8
Cross Breeds - Bonus Chapter

Cross Breeds have definitely become more popular in recent years and they can be perfect companions for those of us who are looking for something very specific in a dog's appearance and temperament.

In recent years, the humble Cross Breed has been soaring in popularity, with many social media accounts dedicated to the lives of Cockapoos and Labradoodles. Although they are 'trending' it's important when choosing a breed that they are appropriate for our lifestyles to ensure a happy dog and owner.

A Cross Breed is when we combine one dog breed with another to create a cross between the two. It's worth advising if you are considering these dogs that Cross Breeds have had better results when the dog has come from pure bred parents rather than parents that are both cross breeds themselves.

THE COCKAPOO

Objectively the most popular Cross Breed to own is the Cockapoo. Taking the exuberant hunting nature of the Cocker Spaniel combined with the versatility of the Miniature-Poodle topped with a glorious wiry coat, the Cockapoo has proven to be the perfect companion for a family home!

Cockapoos are highly intelligent, trainable dogs that live for being loyal companions. They are extremely friendly with children, parents and even grandparents. They are ideal for all age groups which makes them fantastic company for all.

The Cockapoo is a Cross Breed of two thoroughly energetic breeds. Both Poodles and Cocker Spaniels enjoy retrieving and agility as well as learning lots of cool tricks. Scent work such as man-trailing and snuffle mats will also keep a Cockapoo busy and enriched.

THE LABRADOODLE

A slightly larger version of the Cockapoo is the 'majestic' Labradoodle. The Labradoodle is a mix of the Labrador and the Poodle. Labradoodles are excellent family dogs and have even worked as therapy and assistance dogs.

Thanks to both the Labrador and Poodle's trainability, Labradoodles are intelligent Cross Breeds that can be very easy to train. This hard-working cross breed does require plenty of exercise though they are even the ideal companions for activities like hiking.

Some Labradoodles will enjoy taking up agility or obstacle courses to burn off their energy. Afterall, these are very high-energy beings! Both the Labrador and Poodle were bred as water retrievers, so it's no surprise that Labradoodles also enjoy water based retrieving such as dock diving.

So if you're looking for a companion that will be friendly and loyal but also high energy, the Labradoodle might just be for you.

THE CAVAPOO

It's the Poodle and the Cavalier King Charles Spaniel who come together to provide excellent characteristics for the Cavapoo!

They are very good with children and approachable when meeting other dogs and people. The Cavapoo is known to be a very good natured Cross Breed that loves nothing more than being with a loving family.

While Cavapoos don't need as much exercise compared to the Cockapoo and the Labradoodle, they still need exciting and enriching outlets when they go out on walks. These outlets can be as simple as playing fetch and tug of war. Both games create a solid and enriching bond between you and your dog that will take you both so far in training.

Cavapoos also enjoy scent work which can be done through snuffle mats and other puzzles as as well as a good old game of hide and seek. A Cavapoo will get rewarding and satisfying gratification when finding a toy or seeing you!

THE SPRINGADOR

This one is a lesser known Cross Breed, full of exuberance and loyalty. Crossing the Labrador Retriever and English Springer Spaniel, the Springador is a medium sized Cross Breed from two dogs both out of the Gun Dog fraternity.

The Springador displays the appearance of a Labrador in a smaller size, but the strong energetic qualities of the Springer can definitely be found in this magnificent whirlwind of a dog.

As Springadors get older they adjust to the energy of their families nicely with their adaptability to all kinds of lifestyles.

As the Springer and the Labrador are both gun dogs, a highly recommended breed fulfillment activity would be to sign your dog up to gun dog classes to simulate the tracking and retrieving jobs they were bred for. This would be more of a job for your parent or guardian, but I'm sure you would love to hear the stories of your dog's experience.

Your family may even find the Springador to be a versatile hunting dog aligned with all of the best qualities of two very popular Gun Dog breeds. Dock diving, agility and man-trailing are also exciting and fulfilling games for the Springador!

THE BASSADOR

Maybe you like the idea of the Springador being a smaller version of the Labrador, but just can't manage their excessive bursts of energy. In that case, take a look at another less common Cross Breed the Bassador. Bassadors inherit all the best traits of their parents: the Labrador and the Basset Hound. Bassadors are medium sized Cross Breed dogs with the very gentle nature of both their parents.

Bassadors are easier Cross Breeds and will sleep a lot of the day away, which is perfect if you and your family have a busy lifestyle. Bassadors love to be with their owners and will happily cuddle up with them anywhere in your home or in a comfy spot to rest when you are out on a walk. Bassadors are not always energetic at home, but they will enjoy playing with their loving owners.

Some Bassadors are prone to being distracted by strong smells that catch their nose, but dropping some tasty treats forming a trail will build lots of engagement between the two of you. Also, a good game of fetch on land or in water will give them a great opportunity for exercise. Tug of war is another guaranteed way to bring you and your Bassadors connection closer.

THE GOLDADOR

Many people wonder whether to get a Golden Retriever or a Labrador Retriever and what their differences might be. Perhaps your happy medium would be this joyful cross breed: The Goldador.

Combining the Golden and Labrador Retrievers together, Goldadors tend to be particularly large in size and display very playful personalities. They have very dense, water resistant double coats perfectly suited for swimming. Like many dogs, Goldadors are attached to their owners and love companionship which can make them easily lonely when nobody is around. For this reason, they love to be part of big families and are known to be very family-orientated dogs.

Snuffle mats or long lasting chews are both brilliant ways to relieve the initial stress and separation anxiety when they are left alone. Though sometimes overly friendly and a little rambunctious, Goldadors are the epitome of a loving, loyal dog. Both the parents of a Goldador enjoy swimming and retrieving as well as tug of war, which can be excellent activities to do with your very own Goldador. Gun dog classes can also be fun and fulfilling though you may have to be patient and consistent when training due to their tendency to become over stimulated.

THE COCKALIER

If you are fond of the Cocker Spaniel, but also want a dog with an off switch to just relax at home as a lap dog, maybe you should consider the ever-playful Cockalier!

The Cockalier is a cross between two different Spaniels, the Cocker Spaniel and the Cavalier King Charles Spaniel. Cockaliers are very friendly and love to play with their owners, they make wonderful companion lap dogs and can still display the work drive when needed.

When socialised properly, Cockaliers rarely have any reactivity issues or aggression. Cockaliers are very easy to own and can be very adaptable to various lifestyles, making them ideal for many different types of families.

Cockaliers love to run around making activities such as agility, perfect for them to enjoy! Even kicking a football in the park or retrieving games can be fun for the dog and also a great opportunity to apply some impulse control, teach your Cockalier to wait and then retrieve when you tell them to.

THE CHORKIE

The Chorkie is a mix of the Chihuahua and the Yorkshire Terrier, giving you a very tiny, playful and devoted Cross Breed. Although the parent groups are quite small, the personalities between Chihuahuas and Yorkshire Terriers are quite different, but mingle to balance out the humble little Chorkie.

Chorkies don't mind how big your house is, large or small they are happy wherever they are as as long as they get to be with their family! These Cross Breeds are 'clownish' and playful. They love to have lots of fun and do not want to be left out of any activities going on, Chorkies will watch their families like a hawk. Like most children and adults, Chorkies have 'fear of missing out' and will want to be involved at all costs. They have 'youngest sibling' personalities and should be treated as special for them to feel loved.

Despite both parents being confident and outgoing dogs, the Chorkie doesn't actually require much exercise. Whether you prefer long or short walks, your Chorkie will happily take them or leave them, which can be really helpful if your family lifestyle is sometimes unpredictable and doesn't have a consistent routine.

Chorkies are mainly affectionate lap dogs and they adore their owners so much that consequently, they can be very vocal and protective with strangers. Socialising your Chorkie to other people and dogs in various situations is highly beneficial.

A Chorkie will enjoy all the chasing games of a Terrier combined with some tug of war and watching you blow bubbles. Chorkies will also enjoy a run around and chasing other dogs when socialised correctly at an early age.

What did we learn about Cross Breeds?

Cross Breeds can be perfect companions when bred and socialised correctly. It's important to research the two breed parents of a Cross Breed in order to understand what fulfilling activities they love and then combine them all together.

But overall, Cross Breeds can offer protection, fun and loyalty as an addition to most families and lifestyles.

Quiz

What does Cross Breed mean?

Which Cross Breed is the most active?

Which Cross Breeds could be considered 'lap dogs?'

Which Cross Breed struggles with 'fear of missing out' ?

Acknowledgments

I would first like to thank you for reading this book. I really hope you have enjoyed discovering the fascinating origins of so many wonderful dogs and how to enrich them with breed fulfilment!

Thank you Maple Publishers for all the help and support with the book. Also thanks to everybody who provided lovely photographs.

A big thank you to my wonderful editor and dear friend Maisie Hancox for such prompt, skilful and constructive feedback.

Next thank you to my trusted advisor Ellie Scanlan for giving me the best guidance in my creative endeavours and suggesting that I should write a book.

Also, thank you to my Auntie Lynne & Uncle Steve for instigating my love for dogs when I was just a little boy. I love you both.

I must also thank Jamie & Becky Tiffin for giving me such wonderful experiences in my teens, taking care of your puppy litters and watching them all grow into magnificent dogs!

A special thanks to Nikki Wright, Clair Litster-Huckle, Leanne McWade & Lorna Joyce for teaching me so much about dog behaviour. Without you all, I wouldn't have the skills and knowledge to train such sublime K9 companions.

Thanks to all my friends and family for everything you do to make me smile! And of course thank you to all the dogs!

Thank you Benny for being my absolute dream dog, doing everything I tell you and throwing all your love right back at me!

Finally, thank you Max. Without whom I probably wouldn't have been motivated to learn all about dog breeds and behaviour. This book is dedicated in your memory.

About the Author

SCOTT HARRINGTON (DTC-CDT) is a British dog trainer, actor and writer.

His love for dogs began at a very young age when his god parents adopted two Labradors Archie & Barney. He then spent time in his teen years training his own dog Max in addition to providing house sitting and walking services for dogs in his local area.

After writing his own screenplays and working as an actor in high profile film and television productions such as 1917, Eurovision, Agatha Raisin and Casualty, Scott became a DTC certified dog trainer to support himself in the unpredictable nature of show business. Scott's book Take The Lead - The Need For Breed was written to combine his passion for both writing and dogs into one project.

www.ingramcontent.com/pod-product-compliance
Lightning Source LLC
Chambersburg PA
CBHW051416070526
44584CB00023B/3451